A CREATIVE MINORITY

Influencing Culture Through Redemptive Participation

Jon Tyson & Heather Grizzle

A Creative Minority

Contents

"The most eloquent testimony to the reality of the resurrection is not an empty tomb or a well-orchestrated pageant on Easter Sunday but rather a group of people whose life together is so radically different, so completely changed from the way the world builds a community, that there can be no explanation other than that something decisive has happened in history."

-- Will Willimon

Christians, Power & Destructive Minorities

How should the church engage our culture? Many talk about becoming more missional, others about taking our culture back, but it has been my experience that the typical Christian, rather than feeling fired up or threatened by these ideological campaigns simply feels sad, confused and overwhelmed. The recent political cycle has shattered the lens through which the American church has looked at politics through much of our lifetimes. We know biblically that Jesus is the Lord of heaven and earth, and we know he cares about the kind of world we are creating, but those theological principles seem largely disconnected from the realities we face in an increasingly post-Christian culture. Our societal problems seem so complex and nuanced that the answers we have been given no longer seem applicable.

We not only feel this obsolescence on a personal level, but also at an institutional one. Christians rarely hold places of honor or influence in the secular world, and in increasingly frequent cases, we actually hold a place of shame and disdain in the public square. This has been deeply disorienting: America is in some ways a schizophrenic culture when it comes to religion and public life. Every presidential candidate is asked about their personal faith, but if they ever really built policies around the Sermon on the Mount, there might be a second American civil war. Virtually every culturally engaged Christian in America today feels that tension in our jobs, in our communities, and in the broader cultural conversation. Personal faith is welcome, but expressing our convictions or espousing ideas as truth in public is uncouth at best, and often taken as coercive, intolerant, or even threatening.

Society both senses and fears a Christian backlash to our loss of influence, worrying that this backlash will come out in negative or violent ways. Beliefs that were once considered soundly evangelical now appear close-minded and combative. Recent Barna Research Group polls seem to confirm these fears; they report that the two defining characteristics of Christians in terms of cultural perception are "irrelevant" and "extreme."[1] What a dispiriting way to be perceived – out of touch and out of balance!

The further out of the public square we are pushed, the angrier and more frantic our rhetoric becomes. It is as though, out of a fear of being forgotten, we seek to span our growing distance from the center with volume and intensity rather than engaging with intimacy. But if we are not careful, we will not be seen as bearers of good news, but rather as ideological warriors seeking to force a Christian theocracy on a resistant nation.

The rise of ISIS has been shocking and instructive. Their atrocities have been brutal in obvious ways, but also in subtler ways that have often been overlooked – they are fearful of anything that deviates from their own religious power. Beyond their many public executions, who can forget the pictures of ISIS members going into Mosul's central museum after they had taken the city and destroying priceless, millennia-old artifacts they deemed to be idolatrous?

Their fearful intolerance extended so far that, no less menacing than armed enemies, they felt the need to also destroy inanimate relics perceived to challenge their strict moral code. I fear that our angry and even militant rhetoric may cause people to think that many Christians hope for something similar were we to recapture political power: destroy all that is wonderful in the nation that America has become in a fear-inspired rampage to return it to an idealized, moralistic past.

During Jesus' time on earth, the people of God faced a complex and challenging religious milieu. The Jewish people were angry and frustrated at the overwhelming power of Rome and its blatant paganism. Sincere followers of God were wrestling deeply with how to be faithful and fruitful in a place where their values were no longer welcome. Many of those subgroups responded in ways that are eerily similar to our cultural sects today.

The Sadducees made deals with the Romans - they cared about power, influence and control. They broke their covenantal loyalty and sold out to the oppressing empire. They came to terms with the political and military reality, and sought to accommodate it as best they could. The Pharisees were separatists - they functioned as a cultural police and lamented the decline of morality and faithfulness. Through repentance and holiness, they sought to return the people of God to their former days of influence and glory.

The Essenes were appalled at the godlessness of their culture, and retreated into the wilderness as a means of escaping the pagan world. They believed that their secession from the corrupt system would ensure their personal salvation, and usher in the coming of the Son of Man. The Zealots' vision was violent and pragmatic, seeking to seize control by any means necessary, including violence, terrorism or holy war. Jesus Christ entered into that societal melee and frustrated, offended and confounded every one of those strategies. He came in with a different approach and message, one that could be called a vision of becoming a Creative Minority.

I first heard this phrase, "Creative Minority" in an article by UK Chief Rabbi Jonathan Sacks in describing the ways that the Jewish community has not only survived, but also contributed to the flourishing of the world through redemptive participation. That dual focus of faithfulness and fruitfulness is not an easy tension in which to live. He writes:

> *To become a creative minority is not easy because it involves maintaining strong links with the outside world while staying true to your faith, seeking not merely to keep the sacred flame burning but also to transform the larger society of which you are a part. This is a demanding and risk-laden choice.[2]*

Becoming a Creative Minority paints a compelling picture of the way the church is called to participate in these challenging and demanding times - seeking neither to control nor abandon the world, but to love it to new life through redemptive participation. In applying the idea of a Creative Minority to a Christian community, I describe it as follows:

> **A Creative Minority is a Christian community in a web of stubbornly loyal relationships, knotted together in a living network of persons who are committed to practicing the way of Jesus together for the renewal of the world.[3]**

These words have been chosen carefully, and unpacking this definition will be the goal of the remainder of this book, but it is clear that our current vision of the Christian life, culture and the call to discipleship will need a deep re-examination. This exercise should be seen as an opportunity, not a threat. We need a vision that is not based on a fear of a godless future, or a longing for an idealized past, but a rich presence in our own time that inspires the beauty and possibility of Christ's church. The good news is that the church has advanced and borne beautiful fruit in cultural situations much more complex and challenging than our own. The advancement of the Kingdom of God does not depend on the cultural situation in which we find ourselves, nor upon our own performance in response. Rather, we are invited to follow the way of Jesus in *His* great redemptive work in our time.

Let me offer a few words of caution as we examine this concept in the following pages. First, it is important that we do not approach becoming a Creative Minority with a posture of lament. I know that in many parts of the country Christianity is still the majority culture, but this book is intended to be a guide for what the future holds. Living in Manhattan, where evangelicals are less than 5% of the population, I have found this approach to be a helpful way of redemptively participating in the culture in which God has placed me.

Secondly, when we think of minority movements, we normally think of sexual and racial minorities. I believe that these groups give us a rich history by which to be tutored. It is good for those who have had the dominant cultural position to learn with an attitude of humility, and to acknowledge that our dominant posture has often made us arrogant, complacent and entitled.

A Creative Minority: Six Defining Marks

Jesus' vision was that we would be a city on a hill and that people would see our good deeds and glorify our Father in heaven of their own accord irrespective of the laws on the books, the rulings of the courts, or the leaders in power. His heart was that we would influence culture through redemptive participation in the context of communities in relationship. Conversely, He also warned that if we lost our saltiness, we would be good for nothing but to be trampled underfoot - maybe this is what we are experiencing now as His people.

I am not seeking to propose a way to regain cultural dominance, take back our world for God or revisit an unrealistic and nostalgic past. I am humbly proposing that if we take on the posture and identity of a Creative Minority, we may rekindle the light in the bushel, and in so doing, cast a hopeful glimmer on the world.

What would it look like for followers of Jesus to live like a Creative Minority today?

Karl Barth articulated the essence of a Creative Minority in the following way, "The church exists to set up in the world a new sign which is radically dissimilar to the world's own manner and which contradicts it in a way that is full of promise." These two elements - radical dissimilarity and hopeful promise - give shape to the mission, posture and practices of a Creative Minority, which are exemplified in six defining characteristics:

1. Covenant
2. Narrative
3. Ethics
4. Practices
5. Authority
6. Participation

Covenant: Authentic Community over Loose Networks

John 13:34-35: "A new command I give you: Love one another. As I have loved you, so you must love one another. By this everyone will know that you are my disciples, if you love one another."

We live in a relational moment where the needs of the individual have completely eclipsed the concerns of a larger community. The choice architecture of our entire lives exists to facilitate individualism and rather than articulating an alternative vision, the church has embraced this value. We speak primarily of a "personal relationship with God" as the fundamental goal of faith. There is nothing wrong with personal faith, but the love that Jesus speaks of is fundamentally other-oriented and generally communal. If the goal of church is self, we will not fulfill Jesus' command that we be known as a people of love.

Douglas Jones reminds us of the danger of trying to do the Christian life alone:

Followers of the Sermon on the Mount have long noted how anti-individualistic it is. People who finally stumble or are dragged to the way of the cross often attempt to live this Sermon on their own. They might repudiate Mammon and begin trying to deliver the homeless. They might give up on savings and live simply by themselves. They might refuse violence and give more charity to the poor. But in a very important way, this misses Christ's teaching. This sermon is not a code for individual behavior. It is given to the church, and the church has to take the lead in living it in community. People who try it on their own quickly burn out. It is made to crush the individual but give life to the church. One person cannot live the life of the Trinity. The church is the Trinity on earth, and all the gifts and body parts are crucial to sustaining the way of the cross.[4]

God's very nature is relational and so He is best reflected not merely in our individual lives, but in the context of community. It is because of that essential divine quality that God uses covenantal communities to bring about no less than the renewal of the world. Many of us have grown up in relationally fragmented contexts, and we may need mentors from other times in history to cultivate our imagination of what a covenant community actually looks like.

The Clapham Sect is a well-known example of covenantal community. It was a "network of friends and families in England, with William Wilberforce as its center of gravity, who were powerfully bound together by their shared moral and spiritual values, by their religious mission and social activism, by their love for each other, and by marriage."[5] The group's primary aims were the liberation of slaves, the abolition of slavery and the reformation of the penal system.[6] They worked fervently for several decades both throughout British society and in Parliament where William Wilberforce was a Member, and finally saw the fruits of their labors with the passage of the Slave Trade Act in 1807 and the Slavery Abolition Act in 1833.

Because of their shared commitment to one another and these goals, they were also credited with founding of the British and Foreign Bible Society, Church Missionary Society, the Anti-Slavery Society, the Abolition Society, the Proclamation Society, the Sunday School Society, the Bettering Society, and the Small Debt Society. The Clapham Sect are renowned for having played a substantial role in developing what became Victorian morals through their writings, their influence in Parliament and the example they set. In the words of historian Stephen Michael Tomkins, "The ethos of Clapham became the spirit of the age."[7]

The Clapham Sect models well for us what it means to be a Creative Minority. In the midst of overwhelming public opinion in favor of and even economic reliance on the slave trade, they covenanted together to fight for abolition. They were not content with the moral state of their nation, and so worked in every arena available to them to see the reformation of their culture. They choose to live near one another, share much of life in common including rest and holidays, and support one another's visions and goals far beyond convenience.

Having a covenantal community means we choose accountable unity over loose networks. There can be a utility for loose networks as LinkedIn has demonstrated, but a Creative Minority must be built on the foundation of a close-knit community that is both vulnerable with and committed to one another. In such a community, individuals are not leveraging the network for their own good, but rather have devoted themselves to the well-being of one another and the betterment of the community in which they live.

The problem with a loose network is that as soon as there is conflict, people withdraw to their private concerns. If there is no interpersonal conflict in your life, no elements of your character that you are being confronted about, you are networking, you are not in close community. Yet an accountable community does not just confront, it remains united despite disagreements - it is defined by covenantal loyalty. A covenant is distinct from a contract in that each side agrees to uphold their side of the agreement whether or not the other is faithful.

Count Zinzendorf and the Moravians aptly demonstrate what this covenant living looks like and the copious fruit it can produce. Nikolaus Ludwig von Zinzendorf was from a noble family in early 18th century Lower Austria who was set to inherit title, land and money; he could have simply coasted through life as one of the elite.[8] However, he had a life-altering experience with Jesus and he dreamed of becoming a pastor. Taking on such a role was too much of a class demotion for someone of his station, so his family soundly discouraged him from that pursuit. Despite still having a passion for preaching the gospel, he relented to his family's request and took a position as Councilor to the King of Saxony at Dresden.[9]

Part of the fallout at that time from the Protestant Reformation was persecution by the Catholic Church of some sects of Christianity, including Mennonites and Anabaptists. After inheriting some of his grandmother's land in Saxony, Count Zinzendorf offered asylum to a number of persecuted German-speaking Christians from Moravia and Bohemia beginning in 1722.[10] They built the village of Herrnhut on the corner of his estate, which became a refuge for 300-400 people seeking religious freedom.

At first, his experiment was a complete disaster. In many ways, the Catholic Church's fears were realized at Herrnhut – each subgroup had different practices of faith and that produced considerable tension. Zinzendorf eventually took a leave from his position in

Dresden in order to devote himself to resolving the intense conflict in the village.[11]

Zinzendorf began to visit every single home in the village to pray with them and to plead with them for unity around the most essential tenets of Christian faith. In response, the men of Herrnhut started gathering for intense Scripture study and prayer. Through these disciplines, they recognized that their strife was not what God was calling them to as believers, and they drafted the "Brotherly Union and Compact," a voluntary code to which they would all adhere.[12] The members of the community signed that document, which still exists – today it is known in its latest form as the "The Moravian Covenant for Christian Living" - in July of 1727.[13]

Forged in this new sense of unity, Zinzendorf began to hold daily meetings for prayer and Bible study and the entire community was invited to take communion together on August 13, 1727.[14] On that day, they experienced what is called the Moravian Pentecost; the spirit of God came down and for more than ten hours they repented, they wept, they laughed and they celebrated the presence of God. God honored their covenantal commitment to one another with an outpouring of His Spirit and the igniting of revival.

They recognized that the revival God was bringing to their community was not for them to hoard, but rather it had to lead to renewal for others. Just as the light in the Jewish temple was never extinguished, they arranged a system of hourly intercession so that someone was always praying in Herrnhut. That prayer meeting lasted without interruption for more than 100 years.[15] Their fervency in prayer birthed a passion and vision for world missions, which has been unsurpassed to this day. The Moravians did more than all the missionaries since the book of Acts up until that time.

After Count Zinzendorf heard a story about a slave converting to the Christian faith, they realized that some of the most neglected places were the slave islands in the British empire and they committed to missions in those places. In one particularly remarkable incident, two Moravians sold themselves into slavery and went to the Caribbean to witness to other slaves who had no other access to the gospel. They went to the island and soon thousands were converted, as was the case in many other places around the globe.

The Moravians were not only ubiquitous with their own missional endeavors; they were also behind a number of other missionary movements. Their contribution to renewal produced a fruit that was unprecedented for the size of their community. When William Wilberforce was trying to make his case to the Parliament that slaves could be freed and not revolt, he used as a case study one of the islands that the Moravians had visited where thousands were converted and they lived in peace with those for whom they worked. John Wesley bumped into the Moravians in the middle of a storm and they brought spiritual awakening - his famous reading of the Epistle to the Romans was actually read by a Moravian pastor. The father of modern missions, William Carey, walked into the Baptist Mission Society with one of the Moravians' pamphlets, threw it down and demanded that the Baptists pursue the "heathens" like the Moravians.

Unbelievable spiritual fruit came from a tiny community in the middle of nowhere who covenanted together. They adopted this posture of being a Creative Minority and the fruit of their faithfulness was the way of Jesus influencing the world for generations to come.

The Moravians' story may seem like an irreplicable model, but our actions do not have to be heroic or dramatic. Remember that this revival began with one man going to his neighbor and praying that they would be united. He did that again and again and again until the fly wheel of God's spirit began to turn, propelling the community outward in the service of the gospel.

We have often dismissed Jesus' command to love as a cliché, but 1 Corinthians 13 could not be more clear: if we do not get love right, nothing else matters. Yet instead of focusing on love, we keep seeking a more sophisticated influence strategy. That has caused us to reach for the microphone, and the result has been the world sticking its fingers in its ears. Our influence will actually be determined by the level of our self-sacrificing commitment to our neighbors and our willingness to see things through even when things get hard. The impact of the Clapham Sect and the Moravians was not a function of the influence or credibility of their individual members so much as the rarity, depth and duration of their commitment to one another. Ministry and fruit without love is just noise.

"Never doubt that a small group of committed people can change the world; indeed, it's the only thing that ever has." -- Margaret Mead

Narrative: A Compelling Alternative Story

"Narrative is our culture's currency; he who tells the best story wins." -- Bobette Buster

We are living in a time in history that is in many ways defined as "the story wars." People, organizations and companies are competing for mind space and brand allegiance, and their primary tool is compelling narrative. As Christians we talk a lot about how we can share Jesus with others, but if we are honest, in an increasingly hostile world, it can be hard to feel like the Gospel is good news for us. We used to live in a world where it was impossible to doubt, but now we live in a moment where certainty seems out of our grasp. It is increasingly hard as a follower of Jesus to remain resolute about who is the author of the world's story and who we are trusting to narrate our own.

The Gospel should surpass any competing story, but many Christians are only living out of part of the Good News, which gives rise to paralyzing doubts. The full Biblical story is that we were created in God's image, the world that God created was perfect and He loved it abundantly. We were tempted by Satan and sinned, causing a separation from our loving God. Jesus died and rose again to redeem us and now we have the privilege of joining God in the renewal of all things here on earth. Yet many Christians have been taught only half the story – that we were born sinners and our focus should be on getting ourselves and others to heaven. To bypass the notion that we were made in God's image or His desire for restoration of the world is to miss crucial parts of His loving story for us.

[16]The dualistic impulse to value the spiritual over the material is an ancient one. This focus on half the story began in the late 19th century when fundamentalist theologians rose in prominence, arguing that modernist theologians had misinterpreted certain doctrines that

were foundational to the faith. Fundamentalists focused on half the story as a means of counter balancing what they perceived as theological drift in the United States and Europe. We should not forget that fundamentalism as a movement was not trying to put forth a vision for all of life, it was responding in a cultural moment to theological liberalism. Modern evangelicalism is a vestige of fundamentalism in a world now lacking the counterbalance of theologically rooted progressivism against which fundamentalism initially reacted.

		FULL STORY	HALF STORY
Where did I come from?	**Creation:**	Made In God's Image	
What went wrong?	**Fall:**	Sin enters the world	Born a Sinner
How do we fix it?	**Redemption:**	Life through Jesus	Life through Jesus Resurrection
What is my purpose?	**Restoration:**	Renew all things	Convert others, separate from this world, wait for heaven

[17]Because worldview is holistic, we answer the most elemental questions of life radically differently depending on whether we are living out of half the story or the full story of God's redemption. If we are living out of half the story, we miss that sin entered the world through Satan's temptation of humankind; we were not born sinful. Under half the story, the aim of missions is to convert strangers into Christians so we see them in heaven when we are all dead. Not surprisingly, such a missional vision has not captured the heart of a generation. The Bible begins on earth and ends on earth, but if we are living out of half the

story, we spend an inordinate amount of time focused on getting off the planet.

However, if we live out of the fullness of God's story, we recognize that we are made in God's image, and our purpose is to join God in the renewal of all things. Every person has dignity and every job matters because it is part of God's good creation. A Creative Minority has an alternative vision of faith and work that encompasses everyone's life, not just some sort of Christian elite class.

I was amazed at a recent business leaders conference I attended to hear participants say they grew up feeling like missionaries were the peak of Christian calling, followed by pastors. If they felt they could not attain either of those vocations, entering the business world was a last resort so they could at least fund pastors and missionaries. That is not a compelling paradigm – a two tiered system where there are people who serve God, and everyone else serves God's servants.

Some scholars say that the book of Genesis functioned as subversive literature, an alternative story for the children of Israel during the Babylonian captivity. Studying the Enûma Eliš and other creation stories of the near East reveals what an absolute theological miracle Genesis 1 and 2 are compared to other creation narratives. According to the Babylonian myth, creation was the war between gods, and the fruit of that war were tiers of human life. At the bottom of that food chain were human beings who were created to serve the elites. The only people in the Babylonian story who were made in the image of God were the kings and the ruling class; everyone else were commoners designed to serve those elites. You can imagine what a discouraging cultural narrative that would be when you are in exile in Babylon; you are a slave to an empire where you occupy the lowest class on the planet, lacking even the dignity of being made in God's image. To tell this story frees a people in captivity by liberating their imaginations. This story gives them an alternative worldview and an alternative reality.[18]

What a subversive narrative the people of God had knowing that not only are we God's beloved creation, but we are also called as His heirs into the work of redeeming His good creation. It is only when you embrace that theological framework that you are empowered to seek the peace and prosperity of the city in which you are in exile because what you are doing is creating good culture regardless of the society in which you are located.

We have to have this alternative, subversive narrative today. A Creative Minority is fueled, driven, and framed by a compelling counter narrative – the full, Biblical story of God's loving relationship with His people. Out of that flows a substitute vision for the economy, education, human sexuality and many other areas – all of these larger issues fit into this all-encompassing story. How we view God's relationship to humanity and His desires for us changes everything.

Sometimes we can be so obsessed with our national story that we forget to shape our local ones – our families, communities and workplaces. We are called to live out of a compelling counter narrative in small yet powerful ways.

"An essential part of our theological and missional task today is to tell this story as clearly as possible, and to allow it to subvert other ways of telling the story of the world." -- N. T. Wright

Ethics: A Distinct Moral Vision

"I can only answer the question 'What am I to do?' if I can answer the prior question 'Of what story or stories do I find myself a part?'" -- Alasdair MacIntyre

It has always concerned me to read articles about how Christians live statistically identical lives to pagans. It is easy to judge people behind the safety of a screen, but when I look at my own life, what I do with my own sexuality, money and power, I have to face the reality that my life looks more like the pagans than God would like. All of us feel this tension - we are dealing with major ethical shifts in our time in history and we do not know how to think, act and live in light of them. In order for our faith to have integrity, it must be embodied not only in doctrinal statements, but also in actions. We are not only called to believe the gospel in our hearts, but also to make the gospel visible through the quality of our lives.

The people in a Creative Minority are not formed out of the late modern culture, they are molded out of a commitment to the way of Jesus as defined by the

Sermon on the Mount. Knowing what story we are in enables us to respond to complex cultural issues not out of a gut reaction to the world's ways, but rather out of a deep, ethical conviction of what it means to truly flourish in the world.

In his book, *Renewal as a Way of Life*, Richard Lovelace posits that the world distorts "created goods and legitimate values," and that "evil is the privation of good—that is, it is the twisting of some good toward an evil end or an improper place in the plan of God."[19] We are witnessing the distortion of God's creation, the bending out of order of what the world was called to be. It is our job, out of a deep commitment to one another and an alternative story, to begin to use those "created goods" in their proper order so people see an alternative way of flourishing. Rightly ordered hearts lead to rightly ordered lives. When our hearts have been changed by the person of Jesus, the good news of what he has done for us and a vision of the Kingdom of God, these reordered hearts will begin to impact the culture around us.

Sex, money and power are the idolatrous trinity that defines our culture's ethical vision. Where these good gifts of God have been deeply distorted, we have to have an alternative ethical vision that responds differently to and thereby retrains our culture's core principles. Tim Keller aptly describes two ways that the early church employed counter-cultural ethics:

> *The early church was strikingly different from the culture around it in this way - the pagan*

society was stingy with its money and
promiscuous with its body. A pagan gave
nobody their money and practically gave
everybody their body. And the Christians came
along and gave practically nobody their body
and they gave practically everybody their
money.

We need to be a people marked by financial promiscuity and extramarital sexual stinginess. Much like the early church, this reputation would dramatically set us apart from the prevailing culture of the age and would also begin to answer the deeper longings of our generation. As human beings, we crave intimacy, and we have attempted to use sex to fulfill that need. Sex divorced from covenant relationship may feel good for a time, but it does not ultimately fill that space in our hearts. Ronald Rolheiser recognizes the true path to sublime physical intimacy:

Sex cannot deliver the goods; it alleviates our
loneliness too little, especially our moral
loneliness. Sex that isn't sublime doesn't bring
us a soul mate. What it brings is a fix, a hit, a
drug, that helps us through a lonely night or
lonely season, but that, deep down, we know
cannot give us what we need, and sex cannot
be sublime without first living a real chastity.
The person who sleeps with somebody he or
she hardly knows, has no real commitment to,
and has never lived a chaste tension with, will
not have a sublime or profound experience.
Short-circuiting chastity is like trying to write

a masterpiece overnight. Good luck, but it isn't going to happen! Great love, like great art, takes great effort, sustained commitment, and lots of time.

In recent years we have begun to appreciate the emptiness of a fast food cuisine and have witnessed a renaissance of slow foods. It is my hope that people will recognize in love, even more than food, how and why it is made determines its satisfaction in our lives.

Just as we need an alternative sexual ethic, stewarding the power that has been entrusted to us towards a selfless end will mark followers of Jesus as counter-cultural. John Dickson reminds us that "humility is about the redirecting of your powers, whether physical, intellectual, financial or structural, for the sake of others."[20] Our desire to accumulate power for personal advantage aligns more with kingdom of the enemy who used others for selfish gain than a God who gave everything to serve others out of His own power. We are called to use the power vested in us for the betterment of our families, communities and the world.

We live in a world that has indulgence fatigue – we are actually sick of seeing people live for sex, money and power in a constant cycle of burnout. Instead of being driven by sex, money and power, we must be driven by faithfulness, generosity and servanthood. We still enjoy the great gift of God that is human sexuality, but we do so in a faithful, covenantal framework. We still experience the goodness of God that is granted through wealth, but we do it with a spirit of generosity and sharing. We still occupy positions of influence, but we do not use that power to build our own kingdoms, we do it to serve others in the spirit of Christ.

When we bear witness to this paradigm shift, the world will take notice. 1 Peter 3:15 says, "Always be prepared to give an answer to everyone who asks you to give the reason for the hope that you have." Far too often, Christians spend time working on the answer for a question people are simply not asking because our lives look identical to those around us. A Creative Minority displays reordered hearts and lives that invite the question.

The focus of a Creative Minority is not on economic systems, legislation, sexual morality or maintaining positions of cultural power. Rather, the tangible focus is on creating disciples of Jesus in radical community who are financially promiscuous, remarkably faithful and humbly in the service of those around them.

"We must live in the kingdom of God in such a way that it provokes questions for which the Gospel is the answer."
-- Lesslie Newbegin

Practices: Counter-formative Action

I was born and raised in Australia, and every time I go back there, my friends and family immediately notice how different I have become since I moved to New York City more than a decade ago. My values, my pace, how quickly I speak, how quickly I interrupt, how fast I walk – I have been shaped in a myriad of small ways. My daily actions are slowly chipping away at my identity as an Australian and forming me into the image of a New Yorker.

It has been my experience that the most effective discipling experience in the world is not the church, but rather the pervading culture. How exactly does the world shape us into its image? I remember asking my then-eight-year-old daughter a question, and she replied, "Whatever." I asked her where she learned to respond to others' questions in this way. Her response: "Everywhere." It is this "everywhere" that shapes our lives. Christians have been wrestling with the formative power of the culture for millennia. We see this in Paul's writings to the church at Rome. He was asking the Romans to consider the larger forces that formed people into Romans. Then he wanted them to consider how Jesus transformed Romans into Christians. Pastoring in New York City, which is not unlike the city of Rome, I have struggled to open people's eyes to these forces of cultural formation. The French philosopher Michel Foucault called this shaping of people into a worldly mold "the normalization of the individual." Think about how these forces press us into the world's view of normal:

• **Media:** Media is pervasive, pouring story after story into our lives, most of them contradictory to the way of Jesus. What was once held sacred has been transformed into entertainment. In most media, truth has been reduced to sound bites, and the sensational drowns out the substantive.

• **Marketing:** One commentator estimates that we see more advertisements in a single year of our lives than someone 50 years ago saw in an entire lifetime. We ourselves have been branded.

• **Economics:** We learn from our earliest years that more is better, and better is not enough. We spend much of our lives trying to acquire things and experiences in order to feel good about ourselves. The supreme value of life is how much we can acquire. Success is defined by one word: more.

• **Sexuality:** The message of our culture is that sex is purely physical, and that as long as no one is hurt, people can determine their own sexual practices. The rise of pornography has taken sex out of the bedroom and turned it into a form of entertainment.

• **Religion:** All religions are seen as equal and valid, and to claim that one is true and others are not is cultural treason. The only belief you can hold with conviction is that there is not any true-for-everybody belief.

• **Self-Image:** The idolatry of self has gone so far that people are able to speak without irony of "my truth," as if their preference or perspective somehow creates objective reality.

The gospel in many ways is about helping us identify this cultural formation. How are competing values shaping us and how have they crafted our unspoken "cultural liturgies," as James K. A. Smith calls them?[21] We have to be aware of the small daily habits that recruit our affections and become idols such that we end up serving other gods. Richard Lovelace writes that, "Inordinate affection - loving ourselves or others or things more than God - always bends us out of shape."[22] We have to exercise counter-formative practices that shape our culture rather than allowing cultural norms to sculpt us. A Creative Minority is committed to a series of alternative cultural practices that offset the molding forces of our culture.

It is easy to think this happens by information - if we could just get people to believe the right things, then they will live the right way. The authors of *Kingdom Ethics* expose this fallacy in their book:

> *A more sophisticated and common misdirection of theology can be called doctrinalism. By this we mean an approach to the mission of the church, which emphasizes the careful crafting of rigid doctrinal formulas as the heart of the Christian enterprise. This has been characteristic of many branches of the church. Right doctrine (orthodoxy) is carefully emphasized, while right living (orthopraxy) is utterly neglected. Doctrinalism robs the church of ethical seriousness through sheer neglect, imagining that calling Jesus "Lord, Lord," in just the right language will somehow lead to entrance into the kingdom of heaven.*[23]

Look at the amount of Biblical content that exists on planet earth - the apps, studies, translations, podcasts, books – there is so much that we could all be Christian content gluttons. As a pastor, I am in the content business, but information has to be matched with practice or Jesus himself says this creates a culture of deception.[24] In order to properly apply our alternative ethics of faithfulness, generosity, and servanthood, we also need to have counter-formative practices.

Our church hosts a worship time every weekday morning for one hour so that we begin the day by letting God form us rather than being shaped by our jobs and the city around us. It is this kind of daily habit that allows a Creative Minority to reverberate a sacred rhythm that is not drowned out by cultural noise. A common trajectory in New York is to start life in the city and as kids come along, gradually move further out of the city center, ending in Westchester County, Connecticut or New Jersey. Those locations offer more space, better public schools, and a far more idyllic lifestyle. But several families in our church have sacrificed their money and comfort for the sake of bringing the Kingdom of God to New York City. One faithful couple moved with their two sons from the comfort of a suburban house in New Jersey to a modest apartment in Hell's Kitchen where we planted our last parish. They daily make a choice to live differently in order to be a part of God's renewal of New York City.

These are two examples of counter-formative practices from my own church community, but this story from Skye Jethani's excellent book, *Futureville*, illustrates what it looks like to live completely antithetically to the prevailing cultural context:

> On May 28, 1992, the principal cellist in the Sarajevo opera dressed in his formal black tails and sat down on a fire-scorched chair in a bomb crater to play Albinoni's *Adagio in G Minor*. The site was outside a bakery in Smajlovic's neighborhood where twenty-two people waiting in line for bread had been killed the previous day. During the siege of Sarajevo from 1992 to 1995, more than ten thousand

people were killed. The citizens lived in constant fear of shelling and snipers while struggling each day to find food and water. Smajlovic lived near one of the few working bakeries where a long line of people had gathered when a shell exploded. He rushed to the scene and was overcome with grief at the carnage. For the next twenty-two days, one for each victim of the bombing, he decided to challenge the ugliness of war with his only weapon—beauty.

Known as the "Cellist of Sarajevo," Smajlovic not only performed outside the bakery but continued to unleash the beauty of his music in graveyards, at funerals, in the rubble of buildings, and in the sniper-infested streets. "I never stopped playing music throughout the siege," he said. "My weapon was my cello." Although completely vulnerable, Smajlovic was never shot. It was as if the beauty of his presence repelled the violence of war. His music created an oasis amid the horror. It offered hope to the people of Sarajevo and a vision of beauty to the soldiers who were destroying the city. A reporter asked him if he was crazy for playing in a war zone. Smajlovic replied, "Why do you not ask if they are crazy for shelling Sarajevo?"[25]

A Creative Minority does not accept the status quo - through tangible actions it steps into the brokenness of the world and begins to release a prophetic imagination about what life can be like.

Authority: A Humble Alternative Allegiance

One of the biggest generational shifts that we feel in our everyday life is the shift in sources of authority. Where previous generations have trusted in institutions and positions of power, due to abuses and sometimes appropriate critiques, the millennial generation primarily trusts personal narrative as authoritative. In fact, holding a belief in an authority who dictates not only one's personal choices, but also absolute truth is actually considered dangerous; it is considered a "sin" in the modern world.

This notion is so pervasive that Oxford Dictionaries denoted "post-truth" as the 2016 word of the year. The dictionary defines "post-truth" as "relating to or denoting circumstances in which objective facts are less influential in shaping public opinion than appeals to emotion and personal belief." The "post-" prefix does not mean "after" – it implies an atmosphere in which the idea is simply irrelevant.

Throughout its history, the church has undergone cycles of faith and shame. In the Old Testament, the people of

God lived as exiles. In the New Testament, they lived life under the Caesars. In our own time, we need to ask ourselves under whose authority we are living. Who holds the formative power in our lives? If we really believe that Jesus is Lord of heaven and earth, in a culture like ours that Lordship will be tested.

When I look for Biblical wisdom to handle these challenges, I think of the book of Daniel and the courage and faithfulness he showed in the time of exile. In Daniel's day, Hebrew boys as young as thirteen years were taken away from their families and community. Theologically and diplomatically speaking, their capture and exile meant their god had been conquered because all gods were local; if you were removed from your god's context, your god was defeated. Daniel and others were taken away and put in a position of incredible coercion. They were stewards in the household of the King, educated in the wisdom and literature of Babylon and given influence, yet in their hearts they still clung to an alternative authority. Daniel and his friends were given moments of testing and moments of favor. Who can forget their efforts at eating a different diet or the refusal to bow down before the golden image? Many immediately think of Daniel's convictions to pray and the resulting sentence to the Lion's Den. But the scene that stands out to me most is his commitment to speaking truth and his unwavering integrity in the face of personal advancement. Regardless of his situation or context, he lives under the Lordship of the God of Israel, and not the power of the system.

In the fifth chapter of the book of Daniel there is an account of King Belshazzar hosting a party, and profaning the holy instruments used in the temple of God. A hand appears on the wall, and the king is terrified. He calls for Daniel to interpret the writing. Think about the temptation to soften the message and the courage required to speak a word of judgment. But Daniel knows that he is living under the authority of another kingdom, so he does not flinch. After Daniel is brought in to translate the writing to King Belshazzar, we read:

> So Daniel was brought before the king, and the king said to him, "Are you Daniel, one of the exiles my father the king brought from Judah? I have heard that the spirit of the gods is in you and that you have insight, intelligence and outstanding wisdom. The wise men and enchanters were brought before me to read this writing and tell me what it means, but they could not explain it. Now I have heard that you are able to give interpretations and to solve difficult problems. If you can read this writing and tell me what it means, you will be clothed in purple and have a gold chain placed around your neck, and you will be made the third highest ruler in the kingdom." Then Daniel answered the king, "You may keep your gifts for yourself and give your rewards to someone else. Nevertheless, I will read the writing for the king and tell him what it means."[26]

Daniel lived with incredible conviction. He was offered power, prestige and wealth that he declined while still speaking truth to power. He knows from whom his wisdom is derived and has no allegiance to worldly accolades. Not only does a Creative Minority respond externally with an alternative allegiance, they order their internal lives by it. In the ninth chapter of Daniel we read a remarkable account of an angel visiting Daniel to inform him of the effectiveness of his prayers:

> *While I was speaking and praying, confessing my sin and the sin of my people Israel and making my request to the Lord my God for his holy hill— while I was still in prayer, Gabriel, the man I had seen in the earlier vision, came to me in swift flight about the time of the evening sacrifice. He instructed me and said to me, "Daniel, I have now come to give you insight and understanding. As soon as you began to pray, a word went out, which I have come to tell you, for you are highly esteemed. Therefore, consider the word and understand the vision.* [27]

A lot of people focus on the image of the angel, but the most extraordinary thing about this passage to me is the time that Daniel records he was praying. At his point, Daniel has been in Babylon for almost 70 years, yet we find that he is ordering his time around "the evening sacrifice." He had not seen a sacrifice at the temple in decades; in fact, the temple had been destroyed, yet his internal reality was not defined by the Babylonian calendar, but by the rhythms of God that fueled his life.

This is a powerful reminder to us - that our hearts are called to remember and respond to the Jerusalem above, not the world below. This internal allegiance leads to a confident humility despite any particular leader, temptation, or environment that would seek to make us capitulate to the status quo. As the Apostle Peter urges us in 1 Peter 2:11-12: "Dear friends, I urge you, as foreigners and exiles, to abstain from sinful desires, which wage war against your soul. Live such good lives among the pagans that, though they accuse you of doing wrong, they may see your good deeds and glorify God on the day he visits us."

I fear that in our all of our emphasis on being relevant as the church, we have lost our prophetic voice. I am not talking about the church conceding on any particular issue, but the general spirit of the age that wants to be liked and fears rejection. It is amazing how much someone's convictions shift by a simple invitation to visit the White House. Rather than speaking truth to power, we have been seduced by it.

By contrast, rather than accept the prevailing viewpoints, heroes of the faith throughout history have pointed to an alternative authority to govern their lives. I have already noted the bravery and effectiveness of Wilberforce and the Clapham Sect in fighting against the predominant economic vision of their day. When the national church in Germany agreed to apply the

Aryan paragraph to the church in 1933, Deitrich Bonhoeffer, Martin Niemoller and Karl Barth called on Christians to oppose the racism of the Nazi regime and acknowledge Christ, not Hitler, as their leader.[28] Dr. Martin Luther King, Jr. and Rosa Parks were not content with the laws of their land, recognizing that their heavenly authority had created all men equal. Integrity and commitment to another kingdom usually brings conflict, but our lives and the church's flourishing are not dependent on the political leadership of our time. Even patent persecution at the hands of the existing leaders cannot distract us from our focus on our true sovereign.

Living out of an alternative authority means that regardless of the consequences, we are loyal to the person of Jesus. We have confidence about who has ultimate authority in this world, and our actions reflect that conviction. A Creative Minority has a deep trust in the sovereignty of God, the goodness of God and the power of God - that regardless of what situation you are in, God will be with you if you are submitted to His Lordship.

Participation:
Exerting Redemptive Influence

When we think about integrating our faith into the rest of
our lives, "making a difference" or "changing the world,"
again, it is often just confusing. We live with the tension
of believing the gospel is the good news to bring healing
to the world and feeling profoundly misunderstood as
hateful bigots. It can feel like we are the casualties of the
culture war, which robs us of our confidence and causes
us to retreat in fear rather than engage with love. We
want to influence the world around us, but we do not
know how to do it.

The word "influence" is derived from a Latin root
meaning "to flow." This "flowing" does not connote
power, coercion or control, it suggests effortlessness. We
want to influence people by being ourselves, where such
creativity comes out of our community that people are
drawn to it. Redemptive participation means that we do
not hate the world, we are not protesting it, we are

participating in it with a vision of the way of Jesus. Mel Lawrenze further illuminates this concept of influence:

> Influence is not a weaker word for leadership. It is the hidden power behind leadership. We've used the word influence a long time (going back to the 1930s at least), but I believe we have not appreciated the depth of what it means. We think of influence as having an effect, or of getting people to do things. It is so much more. The word influence (influentia) means something that flows in and causes changes, usually a force that is imperceptible or hidden. Influencers are people who lead by living in proximity to scores of ordinary people who are looking for some source of wisdom, discernment, power, truth, and other qualities that begin a transformative work on their lives. Just think of the effect if massive numbers of believers woke up to their potential to exercise spiritual influence in the schools where they teach, in the boardrooms where they deliberate, in the clinics where they care for people's health, in the churches where they serve, in the assemblies where they legislate, in the homes where they raise their children.[29]

There is a woman that I met at Trinity Grace Church, Sara Frazier Miller, who embodies this type of creative contribution. She moved to New York to study theater at NYU and as a sophomore there, she read Isaiah 58 and felt convicted about how she was living her life. She was going to church and worshipping in what she had thought were "the right ways," but she was not spending herself on behalf of the needy and oppressed. So she started spending her free time eating with the homeless people around NYU before returning to her Fifth Avenue apartment. She and a friend started reading the gospel of Matthew and they began to ask themselves what would happen if they took the words of Jesus seriously and did not dilute them.

They decided that the answer for them was to move to the South Bronx, the poorest neighborhood in the United States. The South Bronx has the highest rate of poverty in the country, more than half the kids that live there live below the poverty line. 2/3 of adults are unemployed and 60% don't have a high school diploma; only 4% have graduated from college.

The biggest obstacle to them initially was that everyone from the police to their Christian community said they were crazy to move; the cops told them their neighborhood was a war zone and they should leave. Sara talks about sitting on her stoop one night and watching families walk home:

> *I thought to myself, who is fearing for these kids? As long as they're forced to walk home on these streets, I will too. As we began to focus on being present in the neighborhood, we realized that the people that we were supposed to be afraid of greeted us by name and gave us huge hugs as we walked by. Before long, kids*

were hanging at our house until midnight and asking for food. We realized that no one was taking care of them - most of them lived with one guardian who was either strung out on drugs or worked three jobs. So we started giving them after school snacks, helping them with their homework, feeding them dinner and putting them to bed in their homes every night. All of this was happening while I had a full time job that I not only loved, but I found myself with a huge amount of power, influence and wealth within the company. I was working 80 hours a week, so I had less and less time to read bible stories to the kids or be there for my neighbor when she was diagnosed with AIDS. I had to make a choice. After wrestling for months, I decided to quit my job and raise support so I could give all my energy to being a part of God's renewal in my neighborhood. I didn't know where the money was going to come from, but I had faith because I knew I was in the center of God's kingdom becoming a reality on earth. The poorest neighborhood in America is in the most powerful city on earth. As the people of God, we are called to steward our privilege on behalf of the poor in our city. What an honor that God uses our small acts of obedience to bring his kingdom in forgotten neighborhoods.

Sara's organization, A House on Beekman, provides a seamless series of holistic programs from birth to adulthood that empowers their neighbors in the South Bronx to create long-term change and breaks the cycles of poverty through incarnational relationships. Sara and her team are galvanizing the next generation in one of the most challenging neighborhoods in the United States to reach their full potential. All this came because she and her friends decided to lay down the life that the world offered them to serve the people God had put in their path. They were not content with the status quo of their city, and as a result, their intentionality has deeply impacted many lives.

Philip Yancey, in his book *Rumors of Another World*, tells the story of the remarkable life of Ernest Gordon, who was a British officer captured by the Japanese in World War 2. Gordon was put to work building the Burma-Siam railway through the thick, Thai jungle for a potential invasion of India. The Japanese hated those who were willing to surrender rather than die, and their treatment of the soldiers was appalling. Prisoners were beaten to death if they appeared to be lagging, they worked in 120 degree conditions, and eventually 80,000 men died building the ill-fated railroad. Gordon himself got sick and almost died. The prison camp was a case study of survival of the fittest. People fought, attacked and schemed for the most meager of provisions; selfishness and hate were the ethos of the camp. Then one day, something shifted. One of the returning work crews was missing a shovel. The Japanese guard began screaming that if it was not returned, he would begin shooting the prisoners. "All die. All Die," the guard shouted. Tension blanketed the group. He lifted his rifle to shoot, and one man stepped forward and confessed, "I did it." The guard brutally beat him to death in front of the group. Later that evening, it was discovered in a fresh inventory of the tools that they had simply miscounted. This act of selfless love transformed the ethos of the camp. One of the prisoners remembered Jesus' words, "No greater love has any man than this, that he lay down his life for his friends."[30] The truth of that verse lived and demonstrated began to shake the camp.

Gordon recalls:

> *Death was still with us, no doubt about that, but we were slowly being freed from its destructive grip. We were seeing for ourselves the sharp contrast between the forces that made for life and death. Selfishness, hatred, envy, jealousy, greed, self-indulgence, laziness and pride were anti-life. Love, heroism, self-sacrifice, sympathy, mercy, integrity and creative faith, on the other hand, were the essence of life, turning mere existence into living in its truest sense. These were the gifts of God to men...True there was hatred, but there was also love, there was death but there was also life, God had not left us, He was with us, calling us to live the divine life of fellowship.[31]*

Yancey goes on to explain how the Kingdom of God began to break out in the camp, and in the midst of the hell of war, the beauty of heaven shone through. They started pooling the gifts and talents of the prisoners together to form a jungle university. Gordon taught philosophy and ethics. The university soon offered courses in history, philosophy, economics, math, natural science and at least nine languages including Latin, Greek, Russian and Sanskrit. They built a church as a sacred place for worship. They made their own paint and started a gallery with showings. They made instruments and performed Mozart, ballets and musical theatre. And when they were eventually released, they treated the guards who had tortured and brutalized them with kindness and compassion.

Yancey concludes the story with these profound words:

> *Perhaps something like this was what Jesus had in mind when he turned again and again to his favorite topic, the kingdom of God. In the soil of this violent disordered world, an alternative community may take root. It lives in hope of a day of liberation, in the meantime it aligns itself with another world, not just spreading rumors, but planting settlements in advance of that coming reign.[32]*

One of the challenges for every Christian is that of misinformation: we know everything about that which we can do little about and we know little about everything we can do everything about. Rather than aiming to influence people far and wide, perhaps we should turn our attention to the seemingly mundane around us where we can actually have impact. Several years ago there was a real emphasis on being a radical Christian. During that time, Andy Crouch came to speak at our church. I will never forget what he said: "Being a radical is actually pretty easy; just give away 10% of your money and watch less TV, and that will make you a witness to the people around you." A Creative Minority makes a contribution to the world in which it lives, influencing culture through redemptive participation.

A Creative Minority:
Both Faithful & Fruitful Presence

Because we live in a culture that bows to the idol of immediacy, addicted to spin and opinions in the moment, we miss out on doing the daily actions that would produce dramatic fruit in the long run. The award-winning documentary film, Forest Man, is the story of Jadav Payeng. In the remote northeast of India lies one of the country's largest rivers, the Brahmaputra. Every year monsoons destroy much of the vegetation and homes bordering the river, and one island in the river, Majuli island, bears much of the brunt of those natural disasters. Since 1917, Majuli has lost half of its land mass to erosion and scientists estimate that in 15-20 years Majuli could disappear altogether because the rate of erosion is increasing.[33]

In the middle of Majuli, which is a barren wasteland, Jadav Payeng has been planting trees on island since 1979. In that time, he has singlehandedly planted more than 1300 acres of forest to save the island he calls home. That forest is now larger than Central Park. He explains that he hopes to reverse the problem of erosion through reforestation. The filmmaker asked him if the island could be saved, and he replied, "Yes. My dream is to fill up Majuli. I will plant until I take my last breath. Cut me before you cut my trees." Jadav Payeng is just one man who has remained unswervingly loyal to the cause that has captured his heart. Faithfulness is long obedience in the same direction, and Payeng is representative of the power of small acts of faithfulness done again and again and again.[34]

Every day we move towards the places of brokenness – we do this in loving community out of a story of redemption, with a robust ethical vision, counter cultural practices, under the authority of the Creator, lovingly exerting redemptive influence for His glory. Wherever you live, whatever your work is, I invite you to consider becoming a Creative Minority so you can redemptively influence the world that Jesus so dearly loves.

About the Authors

Jon Tyson is a Pastor and Church Planter in New York City. Originally from Adelaide Australia, Jon moved to the United States twenty years ago with a passion to seek and cultivate renewal in the Western Church. In addition to this book, he has written *Sacred Roots* and the forthcoming book, *The Burden is Light*. Jon lives in the Hell's Kitchen neighborhood of Manhattan with his wife and two children. He serves as the Lead Pastor of Church of the City New York.

Heather Grizzle is a founding partner at Causeway Global Partners, a boutique consultancy that helps its clients communicate, connect and advance their objectives more effectively. Her background includes a number of political campaigns, work in the U.S. House of Representatives, as well as corporate and financial communications in New York. Heather is vice chairperson of the Board of Trustees of Stewardship, and a member of the Boards of Innovations for Poverty Action, Alpha USA and Kids Matter. She and her husband, Ben, have four children and live in Manhattan where they attend Church of the City New York.

End Notes

[1] David Kinnaman and Gabe Lyons, *Good Faith: Being a Christian When Society Think You're Irrelevant and Extreme* (Grand Rapids: Baker Books, 2016), 12.

[2] Jonathan Sacks, "On Creative Minorities" the 2013 Erasmus Lecture, *First Things*, January 2014.

[3] This definition is adapted from David Augsburger's definition of community: "Christian community is a web of stubbornly loyal relationships knotted together into a living network of persons." As an Anabaptist his concern was primarily internally focused. We added "committed to practicing the way of Jesus together for the renewal of the world." This addition changes the meaning and purpose of community to include both discipleship and mission. *Dissident Discipleship: A Spirituality of Self-Surrender, Love of God, and Love of Neighbor* (Ada Township, Michigan: Brazos Press, 2006).

[4] Douglas Jones. *Dismissing Jesus: How We Evade the Way of the Cross* (Eugene, Oregon: Cascade Books, 2013), 125.

[5] Stephen Michael Tomkins, *The Clapham Sect: How Wilberforce's Circle Changed Britain.* (Oxford, England: Lion Hudson, 2010), 1.

[6] Ann M. Burton, "British Evangelicals, Economic Warfare and the Abolition of the Atlantic Slave Trade, 1794-1810," *Anglican and Episcopal History* Vol. 65, No. 2 (1996), 197-225.

[7] Tomkins, *The Clapham Sect*, 248.

[8] Arthur J. Freeman, An Ecumenical Theology of the Heart (Bethlehem, PA: Moravian Church in America, 1998), 234-235.

[9] Joseph Edmund Hutton, *A History of the Moravian Church* (Public Domain Book, E-text prepared by John Bechard, London, England, 2011), Kindle Edition, 130.

[10] Ibid.

[11] J. Taylor Hamilton and Kenneth G. Hamilton, *The History of the Moravian Church* (Bethlehem, PA: Moravian Church in America, 1967), 31-32.

[12] Hutton, *A History of the Moravian Church*, 142.

[13] Hutton, *A History of the Moravian Church*, 141.

[14] Hamilton and Hamilton, *The History of the Moravian Church*, 32-33.

[15] Hutton, *A History of the Moravian Church*, 145.

[16] This graphic is adapted from a paper that Gabe Lyons wrote for Fermi Shorts in 2008 entitled "Influencing Culture: An Opportunity for the Church".

[17] Ibid.

[18] Brian J. Walsh, *Subversive Christianity: Imaging God in a Dangerous Time* (Eugene, Oregon: Wipf and Stock Publishers, 2015), Kindle locations 216-217.

[19] Richard Lovelace, *Renewal as a Way of Life* (Eugene, Oregon: Wipf and Stock Publishers, 2002), 90.

[20] John Dickson, *Humilitas: A Lost Key to Life, Love, and Leadership,* Grand Rapids, Michigan: Zondervan, 2011), Kindle Locations 167-169.

[21] James K. A. Smith, *You Are What You Love: The Spiritual Power of Habit* (Grand Rapids, Michigan:

Brazos Press, 2016), Kindle Location 433.

[22] Lovelace, *Renewal as a Way of Life*, Page 90.

[23] David Gushee and Glen Stassen, *Kingdom Ethics: Following Jesus in Contemporary Context* (Downers Grove, Illinois: IVP Academic, 1994), 116.

[24] Luke 6:46.

[25] Skye Jethani, *Futureville: Discover Your Purpose for Today by Reimagining Tomorrow* (Nashville, Tennessee: Thomas Nelson, 2014), 148-149.

[26] Daniel 5:13-17.

[27] Daniel 9:20-23.

[28] Robert P. Ericksen, Complicity in the Holocaust (Cambridge: Cambridge University Press, 2012), p 26-27. Online edition, available from: 10.1017/CBO9781139059602

[29] Mel Lawrenze, *Spiritual Influence* (Grand Rapids, Michigan: Zondervan, 2012), 6-7.

[30] John 15:13.

[31] Phillip Yancey, *Rumors of Another World: What on Earth Are We Missing?* (Grand Rapids, Michigan: Zondervan, 2003), 175.

[32] Yancey, *Rumors of Another World*, 177.

[33] *Forest Man*. Directed by William Douglas McMaster. Performed by Jitu Kalita, Jadav Payeng, and Arup Kumar Sarma. USA, 2013. Short Documentary. http://www.titlemedia.eu/short-films.

[34] Ibid.